# A STRANGER IN BETHLEHEM
## AND OTHER CHRISTMAS POEMS

KEVIN CAREY

ILLUSTRATED BY KEVIN SHEEHAN

Sacristy Press

**Sacristy Press**
PO Box 612, Durham, DH1 9HT

www.sacristy.co.uk

First published in 2012 by Sacristy Press, Durham

Copyright © Kevin Carey 2012
The right of Kevin Carey to be identified as the author of this work has been asserted by him in accordance with the Copyright, Designs and Patents Act 1988.

Illustrations Copyright © Kevin Sheehan 2012

All rights reserved, no part of this publication may be reproduced or transmitted in any form or by any means, electronic, mechanical photocopying, documentary, film or in any other format without prior written permission of the publisher.

Sacristy Limited, registered in England & Wales, number 7565667

**British Library Cataloguing-in-Publication Data**
A catalogue record for the book is available from the British Library

ISBN 978-1-908381-06-4

www.jesus4u.co.uk

# CONTENTS

Preface . . . . . . . . . . . . . . . . . . . . . . . . . . . . . . . . . . . . . . . . . . . . . . . . .v
Musical Settings . . . . . . . . . . . . . . . . . . . . . . . . . . . . . . . . . . . . . . . vi

Stella Maria . . . . . . . . . . . . . . . . . . . . . . . . . . . . . . . . . . . . . . . . . . . .1
Joseph's Reverie. . . . . . . . . . . . . . . . . . . . . . . . . . . . . . . . . . . . . . . . .2
First Noel Exclusive! . . . . . . . . . . . . . . . . . . . . . . . . . . . . . . . . . . . . .4
The Shepherds' Tale . . . . . . . . . . . . . . . . . . . . . . . . . . . . . . . . . . . . . .6
I Cannot See the Star . . . . . . . . . . . . . . . . . . . . . . . . . . . . . . . . . . . . .8
Does He Know? . . . . . . . . . . . . . . . . . . . . . . . . . . . . . . . . . . . . . . . . .9
Gaudete . . . . . . . . . . . . . . . . . . . . . . . . . . . . . . . . . . . . . . . . . . . . . . 10
Let Us Be with Mary . . . . . . . . . . . . . . . . . . . . . . . . . . . . . . . . . . . . 11
Lord of All. . . . . . . . . . . . . . . . . . . . . . . . . . . . . . . . . . . . . . . . . . . . . 12
When Jesus Cries . . . . . . . . . . . . . . . . . . . . . . . . . . . . . . . . . . . . . . . 13
Offerings . . . . . . . . . . . . . . . . . . . . . . . . . . . . . . . . . . . . . . . . . . . . . 14
Jesus, Born Below. . . . . . . . . . . . . . . . . . . . . . . . . . . . . . . . . . . . . . . 15
Look Kindly. . . . . . . . . . . . . . . . . . . . . . . . . . . . . . . . . . . . . . . . . . . 16
Winter Light . . . . . . . . . . . . . . . . . . . . . . . . . . . . . . . . . . . . . . . . . . 17
Come, Jesus, Come. . . . . . . . . . . . . . . . . . . . . . . . . . . . . . . . . . . . . 18
Rejoice, Rejoice. . . . . . . . . . . . . . . . . . . . . . . . . . . . . . . . . . . . . . . . 19
Symbols . . . . . . . . . . . . . . . . . . . . . . . . . . . . . . . . . . . . . . . . . . . . . . 20
Never Such a Maiden. . . . . . . . . . . . . . . . . . . . . . . . . . . . . . . . . . . 21
A Candle For a Maid . . . . . . . . . . . . . . . . . . . . . . . . . . . . . . . . . . . 22
New Life. . . . . . . . . . . . . . . . . . . . . . . . . . . . . . . . . . . . . . . . . . . . . . 23
New Baptism. . . . . . . . . . . . . . . . . . . . . . . . . . . . . . . . . . . . . . . . . . 24
Advent and Christmas. . . . . . . . . . . . . . . . . . . . . . . . . . . . . . . . . . 25
The Grand Vista . . . . . . . . . . . . . . . . . . . . . . . . . . . . . . . . . . . . . . . 26
The Colours Carol . . . . . . . . . . . . . . . . . . . . . . . . . . . . . . . . . . . . . 27
The Desert Rose . . . . . . . . . . . . . . . . . . . . . . . . . . . . . . . . . . . . . . . 28

| | |
|---|---|
| Look Down Upon the Dreary street | 29 |
| The Christmas Spirit | 30 |
| Stranger in Bethlehem | 31 |
| The Refugee | 32 |
| Lullaby | 33 |
| Sing a Song for this Lady! | 34 |
| Simple Prayer | 35 |
| O What Strange Light | 36 |
| Image | 37 |
| War Carol | 38 |
| Were He Born in Summer | 39 |
| Aspects of Motherhood | 40 |
| Christmas Sonnette | 41 |
| Were There No Snow | 42 |
| The Bear, the Peacock and the Lion | 43 |
| Outback Carol | 44 |
| Come, Let Us See the New Born Babe | 45 |
| The Four Kings | 46 |
| Magnificat | 48 |
| Were He Born Now | 49 |
| The Infant King | 51 |

# PREFACE

Carols are the part of Christianity that spill over into the whole world. Many people who never go to church feel ownership of old favourites. But, as is so often the case, non-believers can be much more conservative in their view of Christianity than many believers who enjoy new words and settings.

As a chorister, singing old favourites in the parish church and sometimes 'posh' carols in another choir, I am privileged to sing in Advent, Christmas, and Epiphany carol services. Over the years I have enjoyed many fine new settings, but the words themselves haven't changed much. So one of the things this book does is to provide both readers and composers with new texts.

Because the story is so briefly told in the Gospels and the number of characters so small, the carol-writer faces some particular challenges: a certain imagination must be applied without straying beyond incredulity; a degree of empathy is called for, but without straying into sentimentality; and then there is the limited stock of rhyming words, exemplified by Mrs Alexander's words for *Once in Royal David's City*, such as: light, bright and night; shed and manger bed; child and mild.

The carols in this volume are set out in approximate chronological order with a few pieces of more general reflection interspersed, with *The Infant King* at the end providing an encapsulation of all the rest. Every time I read the words or hear the musical setting of *In the Beginning* I simply wonder how I ever came to write these tender words during such a tedious meeting at the European Commission!

I frequently have fantasies about preaching, to a packed church at Midnight Mass, that the biographies of great people would be severely inadequate if they stopped at the end of the subject's school

v

days. This is why it is so hard to keep the death and resurrection of Jesus out of my thoughts when writing Christmas words. But there is a time for everything and I wish you joy when you read these verses. Good Friday will come soon enough.

Kevin Carey
Hurstpierpoint, West Sussex
The Feast of St Luke, 2012

# MUSICAL SETTINGS

These lyrics were written both for reading and for setting to music. *The Infant King* has been set in full score by Alan Smith. His setting of its final movement, *In the Beginning*, won the Harold Smart Composition Prize in 2008 and was subsequently published in *The Oxford Book of Flexible Carols* (OUP, 2009). Alan's setting of *Come, Jesus, Come!* was published in 2010 by Augsburg Fortress.

The author would be very pleased to hear from composers who may be interested in setting any of these lyrics. Please contact the publisher if you would like to do so.

# STELLA MARIA

And did that star shine over Calvary
Which lit the Magi where the infant lay,
A distant comfort in her reverie
As Mary left the Cross that fateful day?

And did it guide the angels in their flight
As He lay quiet in the virgin tomb
As it had shone upon the exile night
He left the comfort of the Virgin's womb?

And did it fitly fade before His face,
Our risen Saviour on that Easter morn'
Turning her sorrow with His radiant Grace
To wild Magnificat that he was born?

It shines now on benighted Bethlehem
And on the vastness of our troubled sea;
And, as He is our God but still a man,
Was she the star at the Nativity?

## JOSEPH'S REVERIE

I sometimes forgot at the wood shavings' fall,
As He carefully reckoned the line of a wall,
That an angel had called Him the ruler of all



But I never forgot what His mother had said
Of the angel's request and the price on their head
And I dreamed of stones flying and my love lying dead.



And I dreamed of the slaughter of babes at the breast
And I dreamed of the pyramids' uneasy guests
And from dreamings and angels I never had rest.



And I never had rest as my son strode the land
With a smile on his lips and a staff in his hand;
A hand-to-mouth preacher of royal command.

But the king that connived and the crowd that reviled
   Were as sane as a plumb line and wolfishly wild;
And the priests would not pray at the death of my child.


And the death of my God's Son was for the world's good
   And He rose from the tomb; but I wish that He could
      Have used anything other than nails and wood.


   I sometimes forget with my nails and my wood
      The degree of His suffering as well as I should;
   But His mother was special, so she understood.

# FIRST NOEL EXCLUSIVE!

A labourer and his pregnant girl arrived
In Bethlehem and looked round for a bed
But when the barman saw she had no ring
He took their cash and pushed them in a shed:
"You know the rules; no get-out clause allowed
For labour pains or holy virgin births,
The occupying powers are very harsh.
Come on, you know it's more than my job's worth."

A rumour of the curious travellers' tale
Spread, like all welcome gossip, through the town
And farmhands bored with minding landlords' sheep
Were glad of an excuse to hang around:
"Besides", they said: "We've felt it in our bones;
There's something up; this isn't what it seems.
All of us sleep like logs on the night shift
But we've been messed about by funny dreams."

But they were decent men who all mucked in,
Collected blankets, gave the barman hell,
As usual, called the midwife far too late
But eagerly fetched water from the well.
"We won't take anything for what we've done;
You may be right, your son may be a King;
But working people lose when times get rough
And Herod's rough by any reckoning."

A Commission of Enquiry came along
Said to be clean but in the Emperor's pay:
A senator, a tycoon and a judge
To write a long report to file away.
They liked the human angle as a sop,
Inviting all the media to come in,
Posed with the "Baby Jesus" and as gifts
Left glosses, caveats, IOUs and spin.


And when this cast was finally called to rest
The farmhands laughed at everyone's expense
Watching the barman and the great and good
Grumbling about the rules of evidence;
And Peter liked a quiet gatehouse lodge
But when his Master came to stop the din,
The farmhands stared in wonder when he asked
The barman and the bigwigs to go in.

# THE SHEPHERDS' TALE

The wind cut our clothes no matter how tight
as we dourly prepared for our tedious night.
We checked all the markings and counted the sheep
And prayed that our tiredness would send us some sleep:
I had almost dozed off when the sky came alive
With a noise that I thought we would never survive.

Unbearable light clamped our eyelids with fear
But an unlikely voice bade us be of good cheer;
The sheep were transfixed in an ordered array
As a Heavenly choir sang of birth on that day
Proclaiming Messiah was born for all men
And commanded us to go to Bethlehem.

We didn't have courage to argue the watch
But snatched at our bundles and went with despatch;
A baby was lying in a manger of straw
Radiating the light that we'd seen just before.
We gave gifts and went back to our flock full of fear
But we counted and found that we were in the clear.


There was slaughter of babes and rumours of kings
Which were linked to the birth and our strange happenings;
And we heard that they fled into Egypt at first
So we thought they'd been blessed but they seemed to be cursed:
But as boredom and mayhem went on year by year
The hope that we placed in that night disappeared.


I'm too old for the sheep so I like a good tale
And I heard that the baby had blazed a great trail
From the temple to trial and then to a Cross
And some say that he won a great triumph from loss;
That he was the Messiah who came down to earth
Then went back to where we had first heard of his birth.

# I CANNOT SEE THE STAR

I cannot see the star,
The clouds are black like coal,
Not thunder from afar
But bombed and burning oil:
A child You were in Bethlehem
But mine is gone; remember him.


Born in a rubbled cave,
Swords glinting in the night,
I heard the groaning slave,
The desperate urge to fight:
So many children died for me
And I for them; remember me.


I do not want the tree,
The sparkling lights, the snow,
But Your nativity
And its red afterglow
To help me bear my infant's tiny cross
Through life; remember loss.


The candles and the snow
Are harmless revelry
But I cannot forego
Encounter with the tree
To live my Father's love who reigns above
For all; remember love.

# DOES HE KNOW?

A baby is born
By prophets foretold;
A rose from a thorn
Left out in the cold:
Asleep in a manger
Of sweet smelling straw
Does He know of the danger
From Herod in store?


He smiles at the Lamb
The shepherds have brought;
Does he think: "I am"
Then banish the thought?
Does the gold draw His hand
To pinch Caesar's grim face
And does He understand
Why He lies in this place?


A toddler set down,
His exile is done;
Now in His home town
He contemplates fun:
But as he smells wood
In His father's small shed
Does He know of the blood
From the thorns in His head?

# GAUDETE

In darkening days of penitence,
Before the turning of the years,
We look to make our recompense,
With new resolve and hopeful prayers:
The Lord's salvation is at hand,
Rejoice at His benign command.


Our souls awake in joyful praise,
The fingers of the rosy dawn
Glow in the East to give us hope
Of Judah's crowning, happy dawn:
Where there was sorrow now is praise;
Emmanuel for all our days.


Now may we walk at Mary's side
To help her cousin with the birth
Of one who will prepare the way
For God incarnate, here on earth:
Rejoice my soul, this cheerful day,
Rehearse your anthems, Gaudete!

# LET US BE WITH MARY

Let us hide when Mary sees the angel come,
As she tells him softly God's will will be done,
And congratulate her when his light has gone
On the coming birth of God's beloved son.

Let us walk with Mary on the dusty way
And enjoy the news her cousin has to say,
We will gladly thank her if we're asked to stay
For the birth of John we'll meet again one day.

Let us ride with Mary through the falling snow
Down to Bethlehem where she's been told to go;
May we find her shelter as her birth pains grow
And then kiss her baby, as we love Him so.

# LORD OF ALL

Our enterprises rise and fall,
What once was grand reduced to dust;
Ambitions falter and then stall,
Sometimes deserved, sometimes unjust:
But You are still the Lord of All,
The single point for faith and trust.

Our costs inflate, our savings shrink,
Our valued ways are cast aside;
Yet we still care what people think,
Less tied to wisdom, more to pride:
But with You we will never sink,
Brought homeward on the gentle tide.

Time after time we fail to learn,
As optimism fades to grief,
Admitting wrong, we freely turn
To You for counsel and relief:
But when the fire begins to burn
We flee, abandoning belief.

Through all these failures You still stand,
Our faithful God resolved to love;
For Jesus came at Your command
In human form Your love to prove:
And now the Spirit, as You planned,
Lives with us here, the Sacred Dove.

# WHEN JESUS CRIES

When Jesus cries I hear him call,
He who seeks milk and human warmth,
Who could have been an earthly king,
With awesome power and matchless strength.

I hear the baby where I might
Be deaf to clamour from a king,
For I would never want to fight,
But would console that little thing.

God seems eternally in men,
And so this child gives much to me,
Of motherhood, a woman's grief,
A simple, smiled nativity.

# OFFERINGS

I gave My Lord a manger for His bed,
A place where no-one else would lay their head:
I dared not think they would pay such a price
To bear a child amid the teeming lice.

I gave My Lord a lamb to pet and stroke
As tribute from simple and homely folk:
It would not grace my master's balance sheet,
Nothing but scraggy wool and stringy meat.

I gave a kingly ransom to My Lord
To furnish His escape from Herod's sword:
My subjects will be proud to know they paid
So much to spare a child and His maid.

I gave My Lord bright nails and rough hewn wood
And wept at how my sin was cleansed in blood:
But now our hearts within each other beat,
Our love and sorrow twined so sad and sweet.

# JESUS, BORN BELOW

Jesus, born below all other,
Lowly lying in the straw,
Rich beyond all earthly measure
Yet a brother to the poor.

Jesus, blessed above all other,
Of the Father sent to earth,
You have given each Your blessing
Far beyond all human worth.

Jesus, love above all passion
Who in Passion saved our soul,
Such a tiny scrap of living
Died that we might be made whole.

## LOOK KINDLY

Look kindly on these torn, bedraggled hills
For they have witnessed Heaven's mystery
Of angels singing of peace and goodwill,
A golden thread running through history.

Look kindly on this dank, infested cave
For it has housed the child of Heaven's grace;
No matter it reminds you of a grave,
For such will never be His resting place.

Look kindly on the tree that barely grows;
For it will be the tree of all our trees;
For it will bear the sum of all our woes
And yet the sum of all our victories.

# WINTER LIGHT

When Winter light is overthrown,
Water to ice and branch to stone;
When light is flame on gleaming oak
Stars tears and clouds to cloak:
I know I need You then.

When bread and wine are sacrificed,
Manger to Cross and babe to Christ;
When flesh and blood quicken the soul,
Mother on donkey, Palmtide foal:
I think I know You then.

When stars and candles light the snow,
Shepherd's crook and camel's shadow;
When kings are puzzled by Your mother,
Straw meets gold and wood meets myrrh:
I need to know You then.

Sower of seed, pruner of vine,
Bread more than gold, myrrh mixed in wine,
Light of the world, Star of the Sea,
Starlight on snow at Calvary:
I know I love you then.

# COME, JESUS, COME

Come, Jesus, come: we cry aloud
To bring new hope to weary earth;
We cannot help ourselves, yet know
Cruel death will follow wondrous birth.

Come, Jesus, come, our eyes are burned
As pride and greed shed toxic light;
We cannot help ourselves yet know
Angels will promise heavenly sight.

Come, Jesus, come: our ears are drowned
In choirs of selfish blasphemy;
We cannot help ourselves yet know
Your selfless grace brings liberty.

Come, Jesus, come: our hearts are sore
With beating to the idol's drum;
We cannot help ourselves but know
You are the one: Come, Jesus, Come!

# REJOICE, REJOICE

Rejoice, Rejoice!
Let's all be merry
In candlelight,
Shine with the angels
This Christmas night:
Rejoice, Rejoice
With one voice.

Sing Carols, Sing!
Let's all be merry
In joyful might
Sing with the angels
This Christmas night:
Sing carols, sing
For our new king.

Lullaby, Lullaby!
Pray with the angels
Against the day
Purple in starlight,
Thorns in the hay:
Lullaby, lullaby
Babe, do not cry!

Praise, Father, praise!
Let's all be merry
In book and bell
Praise with the angels
This first Noel
With One voice
For our new king.

# SYMBOLS

The Lord of salvation lay bloody and weak
As the wind raked the hillsides so barren and bleak;
The clouds in the night sky were lowering and grey:
A nail in the manger, a thorn in the hay.

The cattle were restless, the shepherds unsure
As they thought it demeaning to worship the poor;
It was they, not the sheep, who were likely to stray:
A lamb all-a-blemish, the crowd run away.

The purple-wrapped gifts of myrrh, incense and gold
Were the fruits of extortion and violence untold;
Did they visit the Saviour to pray or to prey?
A rent in the curtain, the king for a day.

Yet she saw the star and the light in the sky
As the angelic choir praised the Lord God on high;
And her own special angel had promised to stay:
A rose in the desert, the stone rolled away.

# NEVER SUCH A MAIDEN

Never such a maiden trod this earth before
Never such a bounty offered to the poor
Never such a triumph over Caesar's law
Never such a Saviour lying in the straw.

Never such a servant watching o'er a king,
Never such a chorus, such a welcoming
Never such a levee as shepherds stumbling
Never such a burden as gold all glittering.

Ever is the promise born on that day was
Ever is the Gospel He said would come to pass
Ever is Our Lady queen of Christe-mas
Ever is our Saviour abandoned on the Cross.

# A CANDLE FOR A MAID

Twixt crib and cross
Twixt straw and bark
Twixt holly and thorn
Twixt light and dark:
A candle for a maid
Twixt happy and sad.

Bound gloom and gold
Bound smoke and blood,
Bound myrrh and tomb,
Bound star and cloud:
A candle for a maid
Bound swaddle and shroud.

Raised love from hate
Raised plough from sword
Raised life from death
Raised flesh from Word:
A candle for a maid
Who bore Our Lord.

# NEW LIFE

A new life is beginning
On this very special day;
We are thinking about Christmas
And Our Lord's nativity:
So prepare your hearts and souls as well as your houses
For a new life.


This is the time to remember
God's promise to the earth
That he would send a Saviour
And we are waiting for His birth:
So do not forget a gift for Him as one of the family
For a new life.


The new life soon beginning
Will be full of pain and love,
Of the Cross and Resurrection,
Then return to God above:
So thank God for His Son as our best and biggest present,
For a new life.

# NEW BAPTISM

Thy people wait upon the bank
To be baptised once more;
Discounted now all fame and rank,
All that has gone before.

Those who have fallen on the way
By carelessness or craft
Determined to repent and pray
May take the healing draught.

Restored in Grace, revived in Word,
The water fills our soul,
And so we wait upon the Lord,
Whose birth will make us whole.

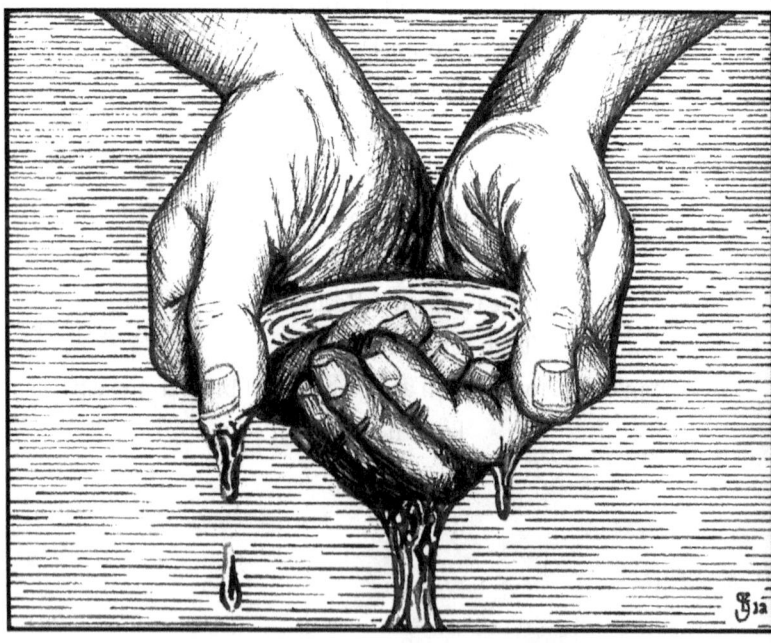

# ADVENT AND CHRISTMAS

The roaring pressure of the world
Invades our inner space,
The greedy bedlam of the till
Reaches our quiet place:
In Advent when we need to wait
Most think that it is here
And as we walk to Bethlehem
Mangers are everywhere.


At this great time of penitence
We need more room to pray
And though we need to think and fast
We rush and feast each day:
The headlong dash for fellowship
Denies an empty place;
But in preparing for God's Son
We need more time and space.

# THE GRAND VISTA

In one grand vista opening wide
We comprehend Salvation's scheme
Unfolding in the candle light
Of prophet's cry and exile's dream:
The promise of Our Saviour's birth
Has brought redemption into view;
What was projected in the Old
Will be constructed in the New.

We shall not mind the cold and damp
In contemplation of our hope
Based on the promise You have made
Not paradigm nor horoscope:
Yet we must strive for penitence
Amid the festive atmosphere
And keep our purple advent watch
Until the red of Christ draws near.

We see the distant star arise
And then familiar scenes unfold,
Of shepherds, choirs and massacre,
Of monarchs, politics and gold:
Yet, in our hearts, we know the Cross
Is standing on a distant hill;
And know that birth and death are joined,
Obedient to the Father's will.

# THE COLOURS CAROL

Red is for our loving Jesus
Sent by God to live below,
Born in humble Grace to save us,
Cradled in the winter snow.

Blue is for his Virgin mother
Who received the Spirit's call,
Shared the pain of birth and passion,
Joy and mourning, Cross and stall.

Purple is divine and human,
Mary mingled with her Son,
Suffering as the way to Heaven,
Calvary for everyone.

Bright the star that lit His coming,
Bright the snow that lay so deep,
Brighter yet the clothes He folded
When he woke from Heaven's sleep.

# THE DESERT ROSE

The waste will blossom as a rose
When our Redeemer comes at last;
His loving-kindness will disclose
The veiled promise of the past:
The exile of our sin complete,
We will return with joyful feet.

The desert will bring forth a spring
That we may be baptised anew,
A highway to our new born king
Will open for the strong and true:
Our strength and truth in holiness
Born of the Saviour we confess.

Where harps were silent they will play,
Where teardrops fell, laughter will rise;
We long now for that happy day
When Jesus in the manger lies:
Then we will dance and sweetly sing
A welcome to our new born King.

# LOOK DOWN UPON THE DREARY STREET

Look down upon the dreary street
With special care this bitter night
And in self sacrifice retreat
From those found worthy in our sight:
May we, as agents, transfer hope
To those who lack the strength to cope.

May we bring light to dark despair
And spread warmth in the coldest place;
Temper the justice all must share
With mercy and the work of Grace:
May we behave as if we were
Those who are lost and do not care.

As we adorn the homely crib
And deck the tree with charms and lights,
May we be generous and not grab
And care for all our neighbours' rights:
May we be thankful for our homes
As places where our Lord may come:

But know His home is with the poor,
His strength most lavished on the weak,
That the new baby we adore
Is yet the servant all may seek:
May we be more like Him today
And smile where we would turn away.

# THE CHRISTMAS SPIRIT

The Spirit celebrates Her child
In silver star and diamond snow
To let her raptured maiden know
How she is faithful, sweet and wild.

*She is the sparkling*
*She is the song they sing*
*She is the news they bring*
*She is the star beckoning.*

The Spirit celebrates Her Word,
Good news in harmony unknown
Which leads the awestruck shepherds on
To see the lamb that is their Lord.

The Spirit celebrates Her King
With gifts secured in rough-hewn wood
By nails of fatal brotherhood,
Sealed with the stamp of suffering.

The Spirit celebrates Our God,
Forged flesh from light's divine desire
Quickening all hearts with sacred fire
To know God in our flesh and blood.

# STRANGER IN BETHLEHEM

**Ladies:** Look kindly on a maiden fair
Fear in her eyes, wind in her hair;
Will he be born before they come there?
Strangers in Bethlehem.

**Men:** There is no room for strangers here,
So full of care and full of fear,
Bide in that stable, not in here,
Strangers in Bethlehem.

**All:** Then in the darkness her child was laid
Straw-sharp; and troubled the gentle maid
Watched as the shepherds their tribute paid;
Strangers in Bethlehem.

**All:** Starbright and sunburst the break of day,
Fleeting repose in the scented hay;
Mayhem and flight as the soldiers slay
Strangers in Bethlehem.

**Solo child:** Infant divine but a child like me,
Here is my gift of a melody
That in my heart you will never be
A stranger in Bethlehem.

## THE REFUGEE

*Inspired by a Christmas sermon recounting the refugee child's offer to keep Jesus warm in the manger.*

Shepherds come with angel song
– In the sky, in the sky –
Of rich for poor and right for wrong
– In the sky in the sky –
They bring a lamb in fear and wonder
Then run away to the dark yonder.

Princes come with cymbal clang
– Far away, far away –
With gifts of glitter, pomp and tang
– Far away, far away –
They half-kneel to a doubtful king
And drop dark hints of suffering.

A child, I flee from my war-torn land
– Woe the day, woe the day –
With only false papers in my hand
– Woe the day, woe the day –
The soldiers threaten him with danger
Let me climb into the manger.

# LULLABY

Lullaby baby, lullaby boy
Dreaming of danger, dreaming of joy,
Which one will triumph, which one will fall?
Lullaby baby, Saviour of all.


Sharp was the message, sweet was the sting,
Angel in armour, announcing a king
Calm was the summons, clear was the call
Lullaby baby, Saviour of all.


Ecstasy blazing, fire in my womb
Widening wisdom, limitless balm
Poured on the humble from this peasant stall,
Lullaby baby, Saviour of all.

# SING A SONG FOR THIS LADY!

Sing a song for this lady:
Hail thou fairest, virgin-queen!
Sing a song to greet a baby:
Hail the king of love serene!

Sing a hymn to greet the shepherds:
Peace, goodwill, to all the earth;
Sing a hymn to thank the angels:
Blessings for our saviour's birth.

Sing a dirge of kingly splendour:
Worship gold, myrrh and frankincense;
Sing a dirge for Herod's slaughter:
Rest in heaven, innocents.

Sing a song for this lady:
Halleluia! Mother, maid!
Sing a song to greet a baby:
Halleluia! Jesus, Lord.

## SIMPLE PRAYER

No maid so pure as maid of earth
who bore the Spirit's child,
who knew the joy and pain of birth
in rapture warm and wild.


Who low before the angel bent,
then answered his stern call,
by humbly giving her consent
to bear the Lord of all.


Who spotless was in thought and deed
and loved her Joseph's children fair
mother of heaven and earth indeed
accept my simple prayer!

# O WHAT STRANGE LIGHT

O what strange light
   the virgin saw
   an angel bright
   within the door
   with God's request
   that her pure womb
   should be the home
   of Jesus blest.

O what strange light
   the wise men saw
   a star unlooked-for
   lit the night
   love out of lore
   grace out of fear
   the lion's claw
   holds the lamb dear.

O what strange light
   the shepherds saw
   an angel choir
   of dread and fright
   proclaiming peace
   goodwill to all
   of our release
   from Adam's fall.

O what a light
   the baby's smile
   this winter night
   his birth we hail;
   we love you Jesus
   Saviour dear
   look after us
   now you are  here.

# IMAGE

The star sparked snow enholographed,
Nature's guile brought to celebrate
A child en-haloed in the straw
In decorously poor estate.



Yet I would take enphotographed
For stars and snow clogged clouds and clay,
A man enthorned in purple scorn
In torturedly rich array.



As snow is cold cheer enepitaphed
Stars map space into time's demands;
But God enfleshed in suffering
Unwinds a shroud with wounded hands.

# WAR CAROL

The prince of peace cries for dying soldiers,
Tangled in war, who fight in vain,
A thorn in the straw scratches his finger
An innocent pang of earthly pain.

Shepherds in barren fields sense danger
And tense as unnatural light appears;
An enemy, then an angel, shouting,
A chorus that calms, then summons tears.

Kings running from guilt suspect the stranger
But sign a dark treaty to survive;
Their gifts of extortion round the manger
The price that each pays to stay alive.

Pain left at the breast of his sweet mother,
The baby can hear an angel sing;
Though sorry the gifts, he loves each giver,
The soldiers have found a new-born king.

# WERE HE BORN IN SUMMER

Were he born in Summer,
Ripening fruit and hay;
Warmed by glorious sunlight,
Lit by golden ray:
Roaming sheep and cattle,
Camels on the way;
Joyful songs and laughter
On the longest day.

Were he born in Autumn,
Harvest gathered in,
Oil and wine of gladness,
Corn stowed in the bin:
Harvest celebrations,
Music at the inn;
Breezes stir and stiffen
As the sun grows thin.

(But) He was born in Winter,
Damp and mould the wall;
Peasants creased with shiver,
Cattle in the stall:
Rotting hay beneath Him,
Rough the shepherds' call;
Wild his mother's worry,
Snow begins to fall.

(And) he rose in Springtime
Blossom on the tree,
Hope in every flower
Life where death should be:
All the earth in rapture,
Love and ecstasy;
An unbounded future,
Life's eternity.

# ASPECTS OF MOTHERHOOD

Virgin mother, sorrow sweet
At the lowly manger laid
All our hope; all sin repaid,
We lay our sorrow at your feet.

Humble mother, reverent peace
In the arms of Simeon lay;
May we depart, like his last day,
In confidence of our release.

Patient mother, suffering long,
Promise of a piercing sword,
Shadow of our saving Lord
In the pigeon's severed song.

Stoic mother, tinged with fear
As the guards with cowards' steel
Forced the prisoner to kneel,
May we withstand the torturer.

Weary mother, sky turned black,
Broken body, promise kept,
In pain He taught you to accept
His going so He could come back.

Glorious mother, full of grace;
An earthly child and pain transformed
Into a universe informed
With the Grace your womb embraced.

# CHRISTMAS SONNETTE

A snowflake impaled upon a thorn,
A diamond of ice in a shell,
A season as close to grieving
As withering flowers on a grave;
A baby exiled in a cave,
A tousle of hay for Noel,
A scenario as far from believing
As shepherds seeing Messiah born:
A blossom of blood on a manger,
A ruby of blood on a tree,
A season as full of danger
As an Imperial decree:
Now see Calvary in the snowy night
And the open tomb in the stable light.

# WERE THERE NO SNOW

Were there no snow,
Although we love its glitter,
Were there no shepherds
To hear the angels sing,
Were there no wise men
With presents bright and bitter,
God is our God
And Jesus is our King.

Were there no star
Shining above the stable,
Were there no stable
With cattle standing by,
Were there no history
But a pious fable,
Jesus was here
And reigns with God on high.

We love our crib,
Its holy ritual,
Hopeful, nostalgic,
Iconic and naive;
But were the comfort
Of the childlike visual
To be retracted
We would still believe.

Whatever fails
We live within the Father,
Whatever strikes
We live beside The Son,
Whatever palls
The Spirit never leaves us,
Nothing divides
The Godhead, Three In One.

# THE BEAR, THE PEACOCK AND THE LION

The growling bear scratches testily in the snow,
The nervous peacock twitches in the Himalayan glare,
The lion of Abyssinia stretches his sandy roar:
Something mysterious is happening in the restless air.

A polymath scratches hastily through old texts,
A nervous priest reads auguries at a gleaming altar,
A prophet wrestles with falsehood's rampant history:
Then each in his own way sees a new star.

One almost loses a stallion in icy water,
The second wrests an elephant from a murderous defilement,
The third makes wily alliance with a camel of no grace
To where the ley lines correspond with the firmament.

A tiny child dozes gently in the straw,
The nervous mother reaches out to greet the dusty Kings,
The whole of the delegation kneels on the earthen floor
And offers gold, incense and myrrh;
Integrity, priesthood and suffering.

# OUTBACK CAROL

I found a manger
In Bethlehem's outback;
I felt a hunger
For something in their looks;
I spied the danger
From the dust of distant trucks;
I was a stranger
But I seemed to bring them luck.

The tiny Saviour
Was sleeping in the shade
Of a makeshift shelter
That His father made;
His mother hovered
Quietly afraid;
She heard the whispers
Of a desperate raid.

Koalas gathered
In a nearby tree,
Kangaroos bounded
To see what they could see;
A wombat staggered
In sunlight blearily
And they all worshipped
The infant reverently.

A helicopter
Hovered then flew away.
They had all vanished
By the break of day.
The Baby Jesus
Was carried far away;
The Southern Cross glittered
To mark where He once lay.

# COME, LET US SEE THE NEW BORN BABE

Come, let us see the new born babe
And be like shepherds, down in Bethlehem;
Angel-song fading, carrying a lamb
To play a half sad pipe to help Him dream:
Sleep sweetly, babe, Your hand upon its fleece
For You, unblemished Lamb, must bring us peace.

Come, let us see the new born babe
And be like monarchs paying compliments;
Yet all our best in gold and frankincense
Ends in myrrh's tears, the tomb's tart eminence:
Sleep sweetly, babe, there is no cause to cry
Until, disarmed, You cry in victory.

Come, let us see the new born babe
And be like children with our bright, crib prayers;
Those simple, innocent desires
Which move Your mother's eyes to happy tears:
Wake now! And take Your comfort at the breast
That we may take ours in the Eucharist.

# THE FOUR KINGS

I gave him gold,
That wondrous, infant Lord
But might have known the fate it had in store;
To be the kernel of his mother's hoard
Until it reached the desperate and poor:
I hear the whispers as I slowly die
That he took suffering for His royalty.

I gave him incense
To make a lifelong prayer
Because the star said he would be a priest;
Its sweet smoke rising in the sullen air
To signify the coming of a feast:
And as I kneel to pray with him this night
I see that star grow black and then glow bright.

I gave him myrrh,
A symbol of His fate,
A gift for one whose sorrow I could see;
And whose trajectory has been both steep and great,
Ending in sudden death, then victory:
For as I read despatches from the West,
They say His followers have been supremely blessed.

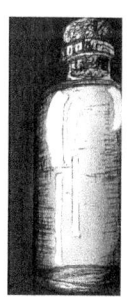

I gave him manuscripts
From sources rare,
Of Greek enquiry and Persian trance
To reinforce the Hebrew love of prayer
And help His messianic cause advance:
And as I cast my final horoscope
I see Him risen, born to bring us hope.

# MAGNIFICAT

My soul lives in the greatness of the Lord
And rejoices in the Grace of my salvation
For He has rescued me from servitude
To be His servant queen for every nation.

All peoples for all time will call me blest
Not for myself but folded in His fame
Which unites heaven and earth in one dimension
To celebrate and glorify His name.

His strength and goodness compass all who love Him
Beyond the ancient strictures of the Law;
His mercy heals all earthly degradation
To liberate the sinful and the poor.

All earthly powers will crumble at his coming
And justice will prevail in every land;
The hungry will be fed, the weak will flourish,
The prostrate will receive the strength to stand.

The promise given to His chosen people
Extends to all the people on the earth
And I will serve them through my intercession
Because He made me fit to give Him birth.

# WERE HE BORN NOW

Were He born now
The wind would have its moan,
The rain lash,
The thunder growl,
The lightning flash:
No sparkling snow
Hardening against the blue,
No frost bite,
No ice crack,
No clear night.


No sun nor star
But creeping, speckled smoke,
The flash flood,
The brown fog,
The blighted bud:
Yet He would reign
From tenement or slum,
The same Son,
The same Cross,
The same Tomb.

# THE INFANT KING

# PROCESSIONAL

Prepare to crown the Infant King:
Though we wear purple at His Court
The time of reckoning is short,
His royal star is beckoning:
Prepare to crown the Infant King.

Prepare to meet the Prince of Peace
And pray that Bethlehem may see
The fruits of his nativity,
That zeal for earthly power might cease:
Prepare to meet the Prince of Peace.

Prepare to greet our Little Lord:
Emmanuel for all our days,
The joyful centre for our praise
Of life renewed and hope restored:
Prepare to meet our Little Lord.

Prepare to love our Blessed Child
Whose humble birth was made complete
When He washed His disciples' feet
Who suffered Him to be reviled:
Prepare to love our Blessed Child.

Prepare to tread the Pilgrim Way
From Jordan's Bank to Galilee,
From Bethlehem to Calvary,
From Advent until Easter Day:
Prepare to tread the Pilgrim Way.

# I. GENESIS 3

For Eden's tree Calvary's cross;
   For what man knew Our Lord knew pain:
   The tree of life, the tree of death
He gathered what the world had sown.

For honeyed apples bitter gall
For what man gorged Our Lord took none:
   The food of life, the food of death
He offered what the world had strewn.

For comely Eve a virgin pure
For what man ravished Christ was born:
   The seed of life, the seed of death
She cherished what the world would scorn.

For Satan's serpent Yahweh's lamb
For what man flattered He was torn:
   The source of life, the death of death;
He conquered what the world had hewn.

## II. GENESIS 13

And through the smoke of wood and lamb
    The angel spoke to Abraham:
"Those who can count thine shall be none
By reason of thine offered son."

"Thy race as numberless as sand,
Thy fortune in the Lord's command:
And when thine think that I am gone
    Thyself and I shall share a son".

# III. ISAIAH 9

Ash glows like blood in the withered grass,
 Smoke claws like death at the city wall;
 And yet we fear more than night's distress
To see Isaiah's prophetic gloom befall.

*For fire the sun*
*For smoke a stream*
*For darkness light*
*Our Lord supreme.*

But dawn uplifts our dismembered hope,
 The sun sets fire to a sparkling stream;
 And we pray Yahweh His word to keep
Of milk and honey in Isaiah's troubled dream.

*For fire the sun*
*For smoke a stream*
*For darkness light*
*Our Lord supreme.*

Sunset like blood but we live in light
The Daystar shines in our hearts where we knew fear;
 And we are wrapped in a tranquil night
Knowing our Blessed Saviour's birth is near.

*For fire the sun*
*For smoke a stream*
*For darkness light*
*Our Lord supreme.*

## IV. ISAIAH 11

A shoot escaped from frost will surely grow
   To flower in unimagined shape and hue
   Changing the way we measure what we know,
Surpassing in our lives what prophets knew.
Cattle with lions, lambs laid down with wolves,
Leopards with kids and poison asps grown mild
Shall not emerge as our worn world evolves
But burst anew, made trivial by a child
Who by the Spirit and of a maid was born,
Whose comfort past all comfort shall assure,
Whose wisdom past all wisdom shall hold sway:
Then shall all earthly power be put to scorn,
The meek raised high, abundance for the poor,
All things e'er known transformed on that bright day.

# V. LUKE 1

An angel tall and bright
    From heaven did appear
In all his power and might
He filled a maid with fear

*O angel so bright,*
*O maiden so pure*
*A soul full of light*
*A servant so sure.*

"Fear not, O gentle maid,
    God wills a Saviour Son
If you will give Him shade
Within your virgin womb."

*O angel so bright,*
*O maiden so pure*
*A soul full of light*
*A servant so sure.*

"I am the Lord's" she said
"May His sweet will be done.
    His servant, yet a maid
I shall bring forth His son."

*O angel so bright,*
*O maiden so pure*
*A soul full of light*
*A servant so sure.*

Then was Her calm restored
That spot so bright grew dim,
    She felt her little Lord
And knelt to worship Him.

*O angel so bright,*
*O maiden so pure*
*A soul full of light*
*A servant so sure.*

## VI. LUKE 2

Thy starlit throne a manger bed
One star alone a heavenly thread:
Angelic praise soft cattle lowing
Their quiet ways the prophets bowing.

Eternal might an infant's sleep,
The darkest night nearest to deep,
Yahweh's disdain a baby crying
His mother's pain a saviour dying.

The crowded inn an empty cave
Adam's first sin a vanquished grave:
The weak whose cries hailed His descending
Shall with Him rise, world without ending.

## VII. LUKE 2

Like coal in light, the sky so bright
    Our sheep froze fast in fear,
      While thunderous sound boomed all around
    So deep and yet so clear:
"Glory to God" the spirits said,
"Good news for all the earth"
Which seemed to be a prophesy
    About a local birth.

Stirred with goodwill we ran downhill
    To find the promised child
Laid in the straw, that infant poor
    Just as the spirits told:
Bending the knee His majesty
    Was never so well hid;
Face to the ground true peace we found
    Just as the Spirits said.

## VIII. MATTHEW 2

What treasure can we offer to our king
Who, seeming weak, is Lord of everything?
No Tarshish hold
Of Ophir gold
Could ever please, for all its glittering.

What worship can we offer to Our Lord
Who gave Himself as the Incarnate Word?
No reverence
Of frankincense
Could ever praise, for all its sweet accord.

What sorrow can we offer for this cor'se
Who gave Himself for us without remorse?
No bitterness
Of myrrh's caress
Could ever mourn, for all its sad resource.

# IX. JOHN 1

Smoky and faltering I shine
　Upon a babe so newly born,
　　And with the new light my powers decline
As He awakes on His first dawn.

Shiny and glistening the star
New born shines over Bethlehem,
But I am luckier by far
Because I shine so near to him.

O faltering lantern, beam so low,
Shining upon that sleeping face:
Who came for us that we might know
In flesh the God of endless space.

# CODA

A dancing snowflake calms a bleating lamb
A star shine cheers a weary king
A berry stores the blood unshed
In the beginning.

An angel sets alight the secret sky
A chorus makes the whole world sing
A mother hums a lullaby
In the beginning.

The snow melts and the star declines
The blood bursts in the gloom
An angel bears a golden cup
On the darkest afternoon:

A lamb starts awake in a golden haze
An angel greets the risen king
A mother feels her womb ablaze
In the beginning.

EU GPSR Authorized Representative:

LOGOS EUROPE, 9 rue Nicolas Poussin, 17000 La Rochelle, France

contact@logoseurope.eu